Are You a Starving Artist?

Antreina E. Stone

First paperback edition printed in the United States in 2013 by
Get More in Life Coaching, LLC
Text copyright © Antreina E. Stone 2013

Printed in the United States

Are You a Starving Artist? Who's an Artist? Everyone
Antreina E. Stone

Edited by Judy Asman

ISBN 978-0-9896975-0-7

Contents

Dedication

Willie L. Stone, a man I would definitely marry again. He is the epitome of the ideal husband, friend and soul mate. I can leave this earth and actually say, "He's never cursed me, only encouraged me." For years he's told me I should be a writer. His words are the seeds planted in my spirit, while my past experiences nurtured the growth to help me manifest my first book.

Willie is the prime example of a God-fearing man. I live with him and I know.

My parents, after divorcing, allowed me to get to know them better than while they were together. As a child and growing up into adulthood, I always spent time with my mother since my dad always worked from sun up until sundown to provide for a family of six children. Sometimes it takes separation to bring about appreciation. I have wonderful parents who used punishment as a way to teach me lessons. If I stepped out of line, I knew what would happen— I would get a whooping. Except back in my day, it was a beat down. But guess what? I'm still alive and love my parents all the same.

My beautiful sisters Dr. Vanessa Ghant, Salena Brown and Deneen Person. My daughter Melchishaua Tycie Person. My sons Darrell Wood and Shomari Stone. The best brother in-law Derek Brown. My beautiful grandchildren, who are like burning candles whose flames always kindle my heart.

Thank you to my niece Nikeeta Emily Howell who kept pushing me, saying, "Auntie, what's going on with 'Are you a Starving Artist?'" Well, now I can say, "Here it is!"

My goddaughter Curtrice Goddard, nutritionist and lifestyle coach. Whenever I shared my dreams with her, she would always say, "That's you! Go for it." My godmother Helen McGary, who is now deceased. Love you and rest in peace.

Hugs and kisses go out to the thousands of customers whose ears are adorned with my earrings sold online at antreinasearrings.com and at boutiques. You are the light shining so bright in my days and will be forever more.

First but not last and everlasting, I want to thank the higher power within me, **God's guiding light,** for not leaving or forsaking me and for budding a new branch, this book.

I couldn't imagine living without His shining light when I felt I had no guide for myself. I know that with continuous weeding, feeding and nurturing by His word, my branches are sprouting to reach and connect many others to the vine—to let everyone know that faith without work is dead. The Gardner has already given you the right soil and the tools you need to start planting and sowing a more rewarding life. **Trust Him!**

> **Jeremiah 17: 7-8 NIV:** *"But blessed is the man who trusts in the Lord, whose confidence is in him. He will be like a tree planted by the water that seeds out its roots by the stream. It does not fear when heat comes; its leaves are always green. It has no worries in the drought and never fails to bear fruit."*

Foreword

During the most difficult times as an **entrepreneur**, I learned how to survive on a **wing and a prayer**. I've learned that if we put our trust in a higher power, many storms will come and pass but we will still be standing.

I built my business from the knees up. In 1989, I found myself crying out behind closed doors, praying, "Lord, if I have to work this hard for someone, let me do it for myself!"

A voice said, 'Sell jewelry."

This started me on my journey of creating jewelry, managing more than 100 jewelry consultants, and selling well over 50,000 pairs of earrings, manufactured by hand and still selling today in boutiques and online at www. antreinasearrings.com.

Recently while kneeling in prayer, a voice asked, **"Are you a starving artist?"** I replied, "Am I?" and **"Who's an artist?"**

The answer given: **"Everyone."**
Then the words began to flow:

> ***The starving artist*** *lacks the ability to use his or her own hidden treasures buried within. They're constantly looking to man to validate them and fear knowing that the starving artist is only* **created by man himself.**

This experience led me to write this book, to encourage others to not give in. You can win. Not just get to the point of feeling like you *fit in* but get to where *you should be.* You have the right to choose. It all depends on the choices you make.

Do you choose to live your life or someone else's?

Writing this book opened a door for me to an entirely new world. I'm optimistic about encouraging anyone who takes the time to read "Are You a Starving Artist?" knowing that each and **every word** is straight from my heart. My prayer is that this book shines ever so bright and lets you know that the power is within you, to shed light where darkness may be and to nurture your starving artist.

Yes you can. You must believe.

I : The Artist's Palette

The artist's palette consists of so many color choices: yellow, blue, red, green, and on and continuing on. Once blended, the color possibilities are limitless. They can become deep, rich and vibrant or faint and lifeless—tons of color choices!

The love of an artist and her palette are limitless. She paints with love, joy and passion, working from images created in her mind and becoming astounded at the end result—a priceless coloring of life.

Your Life's Canvas

There's no difference between an artist's palette and the array of color choices that are yours. They represent life, everything that has breath—every fish in the sea, every bird in the sky, every creature that moves on the ground, cattle, livestock, all vegetation—from the valley to the mountaintop, from the deep blue seas to the murky muddy lakes, rivers and ponds.

Color is all around and not to exclude **you!**

You Have Many Choices

It's you who decides what, how and when in life. Even though we may at times forget the *why*. You can create a life overflowing with prosperity, love, joy and passion while you enjoy the many fruits of life or you can live a life filled with murky, lifeless colors.

You Are in Control

What color would you choose to represent your life right now? Would it be vibrant and full-of-life (fruitful) or would it be colorless? Would it feel vulnerable (fruitless) or invincible (powerful)?

Expression = Impression

What kind of impression are you leaving by how you express why, when, how and what you do? How you express anything is an expression of *everything*—you!

Who's an Artist? Everyone!

Surgeons, lawyers, nurses, teachers, doctors, mothers, husbands, law enforcers, actors, designers, judges, accountants, bankers, psychologists, gardeners, farmers, hair stylists, financial advisors, counselors, mentors, scientists, astronauts. Everyone, including *you*!

2 : **So, Are You a Starving Artist?**

Do you lack the mindset to use your own hidden treasures that are buried within? Do you constantly look for validation from others, not recognizing that you've already been validated? Do you fear knowing that the *starving* artist has only been created by man himself? That you have choices and the power within to change?

On My Knees
I was on my knees praying when asked if I was a starving artist.

"Am I?" I replied, afterwards asking, "Who's an artist?"

"Everyone!" I heard.

This very moment my eyes opened wide and I started seeing the work of an artist in an entirely different light.

'Go Beyond'
"Go beyond," meaning, if I would just step aside, let go of

all my fears and trust the power within me, I would move beyond my wildest dreams.

I must open doors that are already unlocked, cracked open and waiting for me to push wide open and "go beyond" to the other side. "**Trust in Him**, not man. The windows of Heaven will open up with the magnified power within."

When I received these messages in prayer, I couldn't help but raise my hands and shout, "Thank you!"

Thank you for raising the roof off the **Mother of Fear**. Now I'm step-ping on ground I never thought I would tread. I'm now writing, even though once intimidated by the words "is," "are," "have," "has," "I" and "me"—small words that kept me bound from following my heart. **I let go and let God.** He makes no mistakes. We make mistakes by not coming out of hiding behind our fear. I now know who has control. So I've let go and let God. **Hallelujah!**

Fear is Powerful

Fear is powerful but only as powerful as we allow it to be. Fear is energy. But it's our energy that allows it to breathe. The experience I had on my knees told me to let go:

"He will open the floodgates wide, lift me up and beyond the rainbow, which God promised to be a covenant for generations to come. He would be here

and never destroy the earth again by a flood. You
see, when you trust man, he will lead us to the water
and watch us drown. But God, will lead you to the
water and let you float to your intended destiny until
it launches to a full sail, sailing upon the seas."

I believe that this is so.

> **Exodus 35: 34-35 KJV:** *"He has filled them*
> *with skill to do all manner of work of the engraver*
> *and the designer and the tapestry maker, in blue,*
> *purple, and scarlet thread, and fine linen, and of*
> *the weaver-those who do every work and those*
> *who design artistic work."*

You Don't Need Canvas

You don't have to paint on canvas to be an artist. However, you must use your God-given canvas, your life and power, to have everything on this whole earth. Not 10 percent of it, not the west side or the side on which you reside, but the whole earth. It's yours! Genesis 1: 26-28 NIV.

3 : Words

Words are important as well as law. Please read and pay attention to the words below:

Joy, chosen, extra-sensory perception (ESP), grudge, love, hope, faith, electricity, energy, talents, gifts, integrity, trust, plant, grow, weed and feed, impression, passion, grateful, leader, foundation, power, expression, infinite intelligence, nurture, sow, mind, why.

Understanding the Words

Thoughts are words formed in our minds then translated through sound. They can be laid to rest (buried), studied, read and felt. Words are an art of expressing how we feel, what we do and where we are in life.

Words, for many, can be hard to pronounce and when spoken can quickly leave an impression of who you are and where you've been in life. That said, in some cases it's best to keep your mouth closed, unless you want your true colors to come out.

Why use big words when the person to whom you're talking doesn't understand them? Is this merely done to impress? Communicate to create an understanding among two or more parties. These parties don't need to agree, just understand.

(On the other hand, I get a big kick out of talking to myself and I've learned that if we want to stay out of trouble, we must be careful of what we say!)

Did you know that when we gossip, we're gossiping about ourselves? The more we do, the more we become and will be known as one. Words are very powerful. I've been working on cleaning up my vocabulary, eliminating words I may regret saying, knowing that once released into the universe, they can hurt, criticize or compromise a person, place or thing.

I recently just found out the meaning of "son of a b***h." I had never dwelt on these words before. People often use them to express surprise or disappointment. Instead of saying, "What?," they choose to use the other expression. Can you imagine how hurtful it is to call or be called those words? You might think, "Ouch that hurts."

Never Forgotten

Has anyone ever told you that you would never amount to anything? That you're no good? You're fat? You're stupid? It may have been yesterday or yesteryears. Once spoken, you can't take it back and the person to whom you directed your words will never forget. Bullying comes from the force of words. *Yes, words are very powerful.* In the beginning was the Word. The Word was with God. The Word was God. Words like, "Let there be light." Can you see light right now?

> **Joshua 1:8 NIV:** *"Do not let this book of the Law, depart from your mouth; meditate on it day and night, so that you may be careful to do everything written in it. Then you will be prosperous and successful."*

Exercise 1 : Recall the Words

- Close your eyes and from memory, meditate on the words listed on page 6.
- Write down the first words from the list that pop into your head (up to five).
- These are your "seed words" to help you redecorate your canvas.
- Write down what comes to mind afterwards.
- From here, you will start a new painting on your life's canvas.
- Electrification starts now. Change starts right here, right now!

4 : **Prepare the Ground**

To grow from a *starving artist* to an artist who's nurtured and fed, you must prepare for the harvest. You must be prepared to love, sow, prune, plant, grow, nurture, plow, attend, expand, put in hard labor, sweat, pain, create, push, persevere, pray, adapt, choose, plan, seek counsel and transform by renewing your mind and the remission of your sins.

> **Genesis 2:9 NKJV:** *"Out of the ground the Lord formed every beast of the field and every bird of the air."*

> **Genesis 5:29 NKJV:** *"He named him Noah and said: He will comfort us in the labor and painful toil of our hands caused by the ground the Lord has cursed."*

Build Your Foundation

Building a more abundant life based on the simple principles of love, joy, passion, peace and ESP. With these four ingredients, we can soar like eagles and sail like ships. Knowing that universal synergy is directed from love, joy and passion; it can lead us to places people may have once said you'll never see and where you're not smart enough to go. Then, lo and behold, you snap two fingers saying, "I told you so!"

What the mind believes, it can achieve.

Now you are **destiny-bound**, with the peace of mind of fulfilling your life's purpose, living out the desires of your heart and enjoying a more abundant life and the fruits from sowing, planting, weeding and feeding your soil. Your cup is now running over.

> **Jeremiah 17:10 NIV:** *"I the Lord search the heart and examine the mind, to reward a man according to his conduct, according to what his deeds deserve."*

We supersede the expectancy of others. All of the negative words ever spoken against us will return void unto them tenfold. Our foundation is as solid as a rock and as hard as a diamond. Our soil a deep rich color filled with all of the nutrients and power within to fulfill our heart's desire. We just need to get out of our own way.

Exercise 2 : Snap Your Fingers

- Now, close your eyes and imagine everything you just read above happening to you.
- Imagine building your foundation and going where others said you would never go.
- Imagine **snapping your fingers** and saying, "I told you so!".
- Now say, "Yes I can. Yes I will."

5 : Don't Believe the Hype

Not all men are good lovers, are romantic, have a six pack or are well-endowed. Not all women are homemakers, maids, stay-at-home moms, want children or are driven by sex. Not all children are obedient or excel in school.

Many Americans live below the poverty level, struggle with a one-parent household and many live in homes without parents. Not all mothers have parenting skills, love their children or even themselves.

Let's talk about weight. What size are you? _____
_____.

Not that it really matters to me. It's just funny how the media always wants to shove a supersized burger down our throats then talk about how fat we are while our food is digesting. Then, lo and behold, we are now supersized!

We become supersized if we sit and watch television all day long, especially reality TV, not conscious as we load our mouths with comfort food. (I'm raising my hand. I'm guilty).

I'm not hooked on any reality TV shows but am a victim of Godiva chocolate. I have a 60-piece box on my table and when I get to the second row, I go out to buy more chocolate and refill the top row. See, like many other people in the world, I'm trying to kick habits. When it comes to chocolate, I lack self-discipline.

It's OK to indulge but it's not OK to over indulge. Many people are not a size 0, 4, 6, 8 or 10. Nor do they have a credit score of 700, 800 or 900. In some cases, people have a credit score of 300 and are proud! See, there is a lot that goes on between where you started and how you end up.

We use the same standard for everyone. We're only the same because we're human. After we were conceived, while incubating in our mother's wombs, we were called, chosen, predestined and glorified. We were given our own true identities. We were given our own DNA, fingerprints, dental patterns and our palms. When I look at my hands and their unique patterns, a fact of my identity, I know that there is only one of me and no one in the world is identical.

Identical twins are born a second or a minute apart after each other. They may look alike and have the same DNA but their unique identities are within them. The proof is in their hands and teeth.

ARE YOU A STARVING ARTIST?

Can you imagine if everyone had to be identified by a scent? What would you smell like? _____ _____. After all, smell is one of the five senses given to us at birth, along with hearing, feeling, touching and taste.

Think about the keen instinct of animals or someone who's lost one of their senses and depends on smell for guidance.

More Than Just Numbers

When I was born, you could apply for a social security number when you turned 18. To my understanding, now the government hands out social security numbers at birth and when we die, they appear on a tag on one of our toes. One minute we're in the system and then we're out.

People are being fingerprinted daily and someone's DNA is being taken every second. Others take a "bite out of crime" by analyzing dental records. Man cannot change your DNA, fingerprints or dental structure. They can only give you a number.

But numbers don't tell the true story. The content of your character tells the true story, not your size, age, the amount in your bank account or your credit score.

Will your number be the next number called? Now calling number 414,000,999. How unique does that make you feel?

Own Your Uniqueness

Do you feel less adequate because of standards set by the world? Stop! Look at the palm of one of your hands and your fingerprints. If you want more proof, bite into an apple. Let someone else take a bite then compare the two dental patterns. Can you see the difference?

Do you understand there is no one on the entire earth like you? You are the *art of being and becoming* based on the palms of your hands. **Patterns don't lie.** They will either take you somewhere or show you where you've been and, often times, where you're going.

You have the whole wide world in your hands. Do not conform to the standards of the world. Transform yourself by renewing your mind.

You have the benefit of the power within to control your mind, change your thinking and redirect your energy. Take control. Get on the right path that was created for you while you were incubating in your mother's womb.

So What!

Your parents used your social security number to rip you off, you raised your siblings, you lack love-making skills, your penis is small, your behind is too big, you're 50, you've never had a boyfriend or girlfriend, a date or a baby. You're 30, never married, no friends, family or education. You never been shown love, you don't know what love is or how to love. You never met your daddy and your mother left you on a doorstep.

After the dust settles, you're still unique and no one has what you have. There is no one in this universe like you. You truly have **your own uniqueness**. Don't let the brick wall of the past hold you in fear of what's on the other side. You have the armor of your Creator as your protection. This is more powerful than a bulldozer, a jackhammer, dynamite, grenades and a rocket ship. When it comes to the power of God, He will make you an iron wall with bronze pillars. **No weapon** formed against you **shall prosper**.

Don't let your resistance to success dilute your power to tear those barriers down. **You are powerful**. If I may repeat, you are the only one with your genetic makeup, fingerprints and beautiful set of teeth—even if there are a few missing, the pattern is still there.

6 : **We Can Change**

No one is perfect and anyone can change. You and I may not be able to change the world but the world can change you and me if we let it. Feed your starving artist right now by taking your first step toward change or by picking up where you left off. **Keep stepping** in the name of love. Greatness is within you and all it takes is one step at a time. In due time, you will reap the harvest.

Want to know what lies ahead for you? Trust in the One who truly has the whole world in His hands. Many times, when you don't know where you're going, a higher power is steering you. I experienced this when I began to write this book.

In prayer, I asked what I was doing as I wrote this book. I was led to this passage:

*"You do not realize now what I am doing, but later you will understand." – **John 13: 7 NIV***

I stopped asking what I was doing and continued to write this book. **He is real**. Trust Him.

7 : **Second Floor, Please**

You must believe. Ask for it. Follow your heart, not your mind; there is a difference.

Just think of your heart and mind as they are—in two different places. One is upstairs and the other is on the second floor. They're both connected and must function with one another; you cannot function to your full intended purpose unless they're synced together.

When your brain is dead, your heart still pumps, mechanically through life support. When your heart stops beating, well, that's the end of the road. All blood supply is cut off.

Life is in the blood. The brain stem is responsible for blood flow to vital organs. If you're brain dead, you're lifeless. You will not be able to respond for lack of oxygen. The very little things that you can't see are the most important things that allow you to function daily.

The oxygen within comes from a higher power. When

you cut off the power that allows oxygen to flow through your blood to every vital organ, you cut everything off.

Does Your Life Have Meaning?

In order to live, you have to hold on to something. Just a little hope goes a long way.

What are you hoping for?_____
_____.

God made you a promise. Do you know what that promise is?_____
_____.

He said he "will never leave you, nor forsake you." He is with you. Believe it. Keep the faith.

All things are not meant to be seen. But one thing I know for sure, **God is real**. The power within **you is real**. You must use what is greater than you will ever become. If you become one-eighth of the greatness within you, you have become more than what you were becoming before.

Use your power before you lose it. Don't cut your blood off from flowing. Keep it flowing through your body and know that you **can do all things** using the power within.

Look at me, I've written this book. Look at you, you're reading it now. Now, that's something.

I never thought I would ever write a book (my first). This was something unseen. Yet all the while, I felt something deep inside pushing me into the direction I'm headed now. I followed my heart knowing that my intention is to help someone—anyone and everyone—who picks up this book and reads it. Anyone can **do the unthinkable**. When God chooses you to do something, you will have all of the tools you need. Trust Him by getting out of your own way and by following your heart.

8 : **What God Has for You is for _You_**

Don't try to do what other people are doing. Do what God has for you to do. What **God has** for you is **for you**. Let go and let God. Let it go so you can grow.

If I held on to the thoughts in my head telling me how dumb and how old I am, you would not be reading my book right now.

God doesn't always use kings and queens or people with $1-million bonuses. People already look up to them, believing that the rich get richer and the poor get poorer.

If you look at it in a different way, the meek become richer in spirit and the rich become poorer in spirit.

Many wealthy people's hearts are into material wealth and not their spirits. Often times, they have everything their hearts' desire but they're bitter, feeling left alone and sometimes suicidal.

I don't care how large and mighty people think the rich are in the world. To the universe, they're no larger than a mustard seed. A big heart is more valuable than a big bank account.

God uses people like you and me to get the attention of others—not the proud but the humbled. He'll work it from the inside out, getting the attention of people who think you aren't worth the time of day but later they end up saying, "Oh no she didn't!" or "Is that the man I used to see downtown sleeping in a cardboard box now living in a house? How big?"

If they did it, so can you! No vision is too big or too small. You just need an action plan and it can happen.

We are all sinners saved by grace. He knows your heart and what I'm saying. "He knows everything." You can run but you **can't hide**.

> **Jeremiah 17:10 NIV:** *"I the Lord search the heart and examine the mind, to reward a man according to his conduct, according to what his deeds deserve."*

9 : **Bobble Head**

If you keep your mind bobbin' like a bobble head, you won't receive the right message and the nutrients from where all life flows—from your brain stem pumping blood to your heart.

To keep the nutrients in your blood flowing through your body, you must change your thinking. Transform yourself by renewing your mind and confessing your sins. You can live miserably or you can thrive and have everything on this earth, it's as simple as clicking your heels three times and going in a new direction.

Follow your heart as it will lead you to higher ground. If you do something every day, measure it by the amount of light you allow in. This will make a big difference in your life.

Open your heart to more giving, sharing and **living in the now**. Remember, don't believe everything you see. The best things in life are unforeseen. Not seen. **Can you see oxygen?**

Exercise 3 : **Clear the Path**

Let's take this a little deeper:

▌ Close your eyes and pretend you are dead. (I said pretend.)

▌ With your eyes closed, ask yourself, "Do I want to live in darkness for the rest of my life?"

▌ Open your eyes until you see a blurred vision of your eyelashes and a small amount of light. Don't open your eyes all the way.

▌ This is just an example that all it takes is a small amount of light to open the heart to change.

Mr. or Miss and Mrs. Mind

During the above exercise, you may have experienced all kinds of thoughts. Mr. or Miss and Mrs. Mind saying, "I can't believe you're doing this dumb stuff. Open your eyes," or, "Don't you have something better to do?"

Our minds often keep us in darkness by leading us into places we don't intend to go but end up anyhow. But if you think about the word "anyhow" it's like "anybody" and can apply to everybody. It's like opening your arms wide and saying, "Come one. Come all."

We all have a conscious and subconscious mind. But it's the superconscious with which we want to be in tune. The subconscious mind is there but not there. That's why it's sub. It's deep within the mind, processing everything of which you're not aware. It operates the same as the CIA, FBI or a private investigator. It secretly gathers information about you, including what you're consciously aware of, accumulating all of your life experiences from birth until now.

Right now, you **have full control** to function like someone full of light. You have the power to control your mind. Lightness and darkness cannot mix. If you think about the moon and the stars at night, they sit there bright for all to see. They were given to us as a guide, to shine just a little light so we can see where we're going at night.

In some areas, there are no street lights, nada. But that little twinkling little star and the moon are there to help guide us through the darkness into the marvelous light. It doesn't matter where we are, the stars and the moon only come out at night. Along with werewolves and freaks. I'm just saying :-).

When darkness starts to come in, it appears the sun is going down even though the sun is actually staying up. As darkness starts to take over, the sun radiates with vibrant colors—yellow mixed with red to create orange and many more unbelievable awesome colors. Colors we may not even be able to create by mixing paint. That's how darkness takes over, by capturing us with the appearance of beautiful colors until the true colors start showing, turning to pure darkness. It's beautiful when the day comes to sunset. How beautiful is it? When the sun rises and sets, it stays on our minds and in our hearts each day.

Is the picture in your mind as bright and colorful? I hope this book sheds light on how darkness can take over just a little light and how a little light can overpower darkness. When the sun begins to rise, the colors are still radiant but not as deep and at the same time, it's still dark. Then, lo and behold, we blink and then it's totally daylight.

Light = Oxygen

In the beginning God's spirit hovered over the darkness of the earth. Everything was dark. "He said let there be light." Everything has a beginning and an end. Everything that has breath needs oxygen. God formed the first man from the ground. He then breathed into his mouth to give him life. God's breath is the oxygen. We cannot live without oxygen. It's needed to fully function. Every day, always, for the rest of our lives.

10 : **Let It Go So You Can Flow**

Many walk around in darkness with their eyes open, crying, lying, pretending, pointing their fingers at someone else—forgetting there are three fingers pointing back at them. Everyone is to blame except themselves. Their mother was on drugs, they were in an orphanage.

It's often been said, "I don't know my daddy."

Have you ever thought that maybe your daddy didn't want to know you? Who's to say that by knowing your daddy, momma and other family members, by getting a job and so on, your life would have been better?

It's the sub our minds hold on to as opposed to the superconscious. The sub of our minds causes us to stay in one place by keeping us gagged, tied up and cold-hearted to things we experienced long ago. We refuse to let love in or out. Our hearts are hardened like clay soil, clogging our arteries and blocking our oxygen from flowing 100 percent. We continue to suffocate and stumble in darkness, not allowing the energy of the superconscious to guide us away from a dark past. We continue to allow ourselves to be consumed by the smog.

My father told me many times, "Sweep around your own front door, before you sweep around mine."

Exercise 4 : From Darkness to Llght

- May I ask you to close your eyes once again? Please do so for a
  few minutes.

- On a piece of paper, write down all the thoughts you have while your eyes were closed. Get another piece of paper if you need to.

- After writing down your thoughts, look at them. Ask yourself, "Am I going to let these little thoughts and words cast darkness over the light I do have?" The light that's been knocking on your heart, wanting your attention.

- Replace the negative words with positive words. Artists only use interpretations of the colors they see while the true colors shine through! Paint a brighter future. Nurture your starving artist. Let the sun rise and shine through you. Cast out the darkness that's keeping you from moving forward?

Out of Your Head

Let's look at the above exercise another way. These thoughts are now out of your head and on paper.

I'm not sure if you believe in a higher power. May I ask, do you?

Surprisingly, by doing the above exercise, you just tapped into your power within. You had to have the strength to write your deepest, darkest thoughts down. This strength is connected to **your power** within, giving you courage to face these thoughts.

You will no longer battle with those thoughts going on inside your head. Instead, you slayed them out of your mind, one by one, writing them down, staring at them and saying, "No more! I'm done with this. What can I do to change it? "

It took courage to do what you just did. **High five to you!**

11 : **Bound by Our Thoughts**

Often times we're held in bondage by our thoughts. Everything we see, hear and talk about becomes a part of us. What we say and think is who we really are. We're all artists, each and every one of us. It's how we express what we do that leaves an impression of who we are and how we do what we do. It's simply the art of being.

Spinning Round

Remember not to let your thoughts cause you to spin around in circles without your having control over your life. Instead, write your thoughts down. Replace the negative words with positive words.

Use your power within to stare those uncontrollable thoughts in the face, making you conscious of your actions.

Once you do that, you can start in a new direction. Just like what you experienced.

Exercise 5 : Click Your Heels

Caution: Do this exercise in a wide open space. Safety first.

- Stand up.
- Click your heels three times. Start turning around, then keep turning around.
- Stop right before you start feeling dizzy and while you can stand without falling over.
- You may need to hold on to something when you're done turning, holding on and hoping you don't fall are all you need to keep you from falling.
- When you stop spinning, you'll be headed in a new direction and you should not be standing where you started. If not, spin again!

An artist only uses an interpretation of the color they see, while the true colors are shining through!

Jeremiah 4: 14 NIV: *"O Jerusalem, wash the evil from your heart and be saved. How long will you harbor wicked thoughts?"*

12 : Can You See the Forest for the Trees?

I just finished baking a cake. I asked my husband, "What does, 'You can't see the forest for the trees,' mean to you?"

"You need to step back and look at the bigger picture," he replied.

"A forest is a place for the wild and all of nature. Where trees bind and intertwine close together," I said.

Clear Away the Weeds

If we look beyond the trees, you see more than just trees. We see the actual beauty of the forest. Birds, squirrels, wild vines and wild animals. If we look at the tallest tree with the biggest trunk, does that mean it's been there the longest?

Can we compare a forest to a place deep within our minds where there are a lot of trees for thoughts intertwined? Now the forest is in our heads. If we clear the trees from the forest, would there still be a forest?

What about if we clear away the weeds that eat away at our **trees for thought?**

This way, we can focus on our trees—big trees with the deepest roots and large trunks, the trees that add value, ignite love, passion and joy. At the same time we can nurture the smaller trees that add to our growth. Wouldn't we have a beautiful forest filled with budding thoughts?

There's nothing like seeing a huge tree, tall with big trunks, tons of branches, budding everywhere with roots so deep. Instead of breaking off, its branches bud and cause new trees to sprout and grow, intertwining to remain in the vine.

> **The Gardner: John 15: 1-8 NIV:** *"I am the true vine, and my Father is the gardener. He cuts off every branch in me that bears no fruit, while every branch that does bear fruit he prunes so that it will be even more fruitful. You are already clean because of the word I have spoken to you. Remain in me, as I also remain in you. No branch can bear fruit by itself; it must remain in the vine. Neither can you bear fruit unless you remain in me.*
>
> *"I am the vine; you are the branches. If you remain in me and I in you, you will bear much fruit; apart from me you can do nothing. If you*

*do not remain in me, you are like a branch that
is thrown away and withers; such branches are
picked up, thrown into the fire and burned. If you
remain in me and my words remain in you, ask
whatever you wish, and it will be done for you. This
is to my Father's glory, that you bear much fruit,
showing yourselves to be my disciples."*

Forest of Thoughts

There is **something in the forest** for all of us. If we take our biggest dreams or wishes out of our head and write them down while wholeheartedly focusing on the thoughts with the deepest roots and those with smaller roots that will add value, we will remain in the vine. We can sow, prune and nurture these thoughts until they fully manifest. This is the only way we will be able to see the forest.

In our minds, we hold **our wildest dreams**. Until we take time to feed our minds, properly nurture our thoughts and allow our self-discipline to be in control, we will leave this earth not living our wildest dreams. The universe is here for us to have everything in it.

- What are your biggest dreams?
- What tree for thought has the biggest roots for you?
- Will the roots remain in the vine?

The Gardner

The Gardner will give you every tool you need for mastering your life. We need to remain in the vine and not on it. The trees for thoughts on which we constantly feed but not nurture are merely wishes, allowing other trees to grow and build walls of fear so that we don't see the whole picture. It's time to cut down those trees of thoughts that are holding you back. It's time to step back and look at the bigger picture.

> **Genesis 2: 9 NIV:** *"And the God Lord made all kinds of trees grow out of the ground—trees that were pleasing to the eye and good for food. In the middle of the garden were the tree of life and the tree of knowledge of good and evil."*

13 : Storms

If you ever feel like you're lost in a storm, well click your heels three times to return home. Everyone has been caught in a storm. What kind? Really, does it matter if it's rain, wind, hell, finances, work, family, relationships and self? With many more that we can add. The point is to attempt to eliminate as many storms from happening in our lives.

We cannot control storms caused by Mother Nature. The best we can do is take shelter and find the best way to get away.

We always know when storms are on the way. The warning bells are there whether we choose to hear them or not. We receive text messages, read updates in social media, watch breaking news on TV and get calls from friends and family members, gossiping and maybe even creating new storms.

Then there are other types of storms, the storms we can create and avoid. We always know when they're coming too whether we're conscious of it or not. Have you heard of a quiet storm? Do you think there's such a thing? Quiet storms exist when we don't put the why in choices we make.

Think back to decisions you've made. Maybe at the time, you thought you were making the right decision. Later down the road, a hell storm came along and blew the roof from your nestled shelter.

We create quiet storms when we don't first ask why we're doing something; our intentions become the result of the "how," "where" and "what." During storms, if we sit and calm ourselves before making a decision, instead of making a decision that will create new, disastrous storm, we will be able to see the "why." This will lead us to the result we want.

Always remember a ship sails best in calm waters. Be still and calm so that you hear the **quiet voice within**. This voice is giving you the power to quiet and do away with all storms. The lesson, trust Him. Do not lose your hope when things don't go your way. Right now, I'm pointing at everyone including myself.

Set Yourself Free

If, we're going to be true to ourselves, we must admit to our faults. When we woman up or man up, accept our lessons and learn from our trials, we confront ourselves by removing the chains and ropes within that hold us captive.

The Creator gave us a simple way out of everything, it's just like clicking our heels three times. Admitting and confessing to the truth shall set us free.

> **Acts 24:14 NIV:** *"Then will I also **confess** to thee that thy own right hand can save thee. Then I will also **admit** to you that your own right hand can save you."*

So let's agree to admit our sins to each other and pray for each other. Confess our faults one to another, and pray one for another, "that ye may be healed," James 5:16 NIV.

Do you know how many people walk around surrounded by a shadow of darkness simply because they won't confess that something is their fault? Do you know how many heart attacks, strokes, cases of high blood pressure, suicides and loony tunes are out there? We all make what we call mistakes, wrong decisions. Let me turn this around and say,

We all create lessons during our life time, showing and teaching us the right way or no way.

At times, when we're going the *right way*, we get caught up and don't see that we're on the right track. Then we may choose the other way—the way we should not have chosen. Because we choose this way, little storms quietly creep up, remaining there ignored until the winds of the "quiet storm" get strong enough to grab our attention.

If we sit back and look at some of our past storms, weed out the bad and store up the good, then we can say, "Lesson well learned!"

Don't Lose Yourself

Don't lose yourself to storms. That's just what they are, storms. Perhaps there were times in our lives when a small, yes, storm turned into a big no-no. We all try not to make mistakes. But all of those lessons are there to strengthen us.

Storms are a reaction of an action or the result of what we see outside of our windows. In other words, doing what others think we should do. If you find yourself caught in a storm, choose to stay on your path or pull over (pause, do nothing) and wait until the storm lightens up. While waiting, we often find ourselves quiet and in deep thought. I call this "training time." Learn from the storm and move on. Brighter days are ahead.

Follow Instructions

Nothing stays the same in our lives and yet we try to hold on to everything. By not letting go, we allow ourselves to be in everlasting storms.

In biblical days, it rained for 40 days and 40 nights, everything that had breath, all of the vegetation, were wiped out, except for the creatures that were on Noah's ark. If Noah had been afraid to let the dove fly out to see if the water had receded, he would have never known that it would be OK to exit the ark.

You see, prior to the storm, God gave Noah a message to build an ark, giving him instructions on how to build it and what to put on it. Believe it or not, when a storm is coming, the power within is guiding us on what to do. However, often times, we ignore our hearts and carry on with what we're doing, acting on what's inside our heads.

Just think about what would have happened if Noah ignored his intuition, the power within. Earth would have been destroyed. What was the result of Noah following his heart? He was able to continue on with his life, saving men, women, creatures that move along the ground, birds of the air and every kind of food that could be eaten and stored away. Therefore Earth's habitation could continue to be fruitful and multiply, despite the storm.

Even though the storm was destroying everything outside the ark, Noah saved other creatures. Can you imagine someone saying to you, "God will destroy the earth. I want to save you. I'm building an ark to protect us, come and join me."?

You're probably replying to this before even thinking about it. This reminds me of something my 11-year old grandson Tyrell Wood said to me one day, "Grandma **think twice** and act once." I've since used his advice quite often. Some things in life warrant a quick response, like saying "no" to drugs and "yes" to a glass of red wine. Noah removed all self-doubt, never allowing fear to tell him that he was crazy to try and save two of every living on earth.

Man creates his own lack. We harden our hearts like Pharaoh when he was told to let the people go and he didn't. Look at the storms he created. He lost a son, vegetation, and water (just to name a few). If you haven't read it, I encourage you to take the time to read this scripture in the bible or watch "The Ten Commandments." You'll see how many storms were created because the children of Israel lost their faith; they complained there was no God and built their own false god made of gold.

During storms, you must find ways to float and not drown in the sea of darkness. **It's OK to make mistakes.** If you don't make them, you'll never strengthen your power to find the *right way* when you don't know what to do.

The Creator admitted that never again will all life be cut off by waters of a flood. It was apparently a wet mess! Instead, He promised all generations to come that He would set His rainbow in the clouds as a reminder of His promise to us.

The next time you see a rainbow, remember that His promise is real. He also promised to never leave you or forsake you. Trust Him!

What promises have you kept?

What do you use to remind yourself of your promises?

An experience in our lives can lead us to make promises to ourselves, just like the flood. How many times have we said, "I will never **do that again**." But we do it anyway.

Think deeply about what changes you can make right now to allow you to move toward more peace, love, joy and happiness in your life.

Exercise 6 : What's Missing?

- Let's make a promise to each other: My promise to you is I will no longer create my own storms if you promise the same to me. My book can be my covenant to you, a reminder to always listen and follow my heart and be guided by the power within, therefore being able to float and weather the storms if need be.

- What will you use to remind you of our promise? Please email your answer to info@ getmoreinlifecoaching.com or by visiting getmoreinlifecoaching.com to leave your comment.

14 : **Death of a Kiss**

When we meet and greet someone, we speak, wave, nod, stare, hug, extend our hands, kiss or just be silent. Can you recall how you were last greeted? Did you use any of the above options? If not what was your choice?

Have you ever been greeted with a kiss? Do remember how it felt? I wonder why people hug and kiss you even if they really didn't want to. You must remember to not do things you think will make someone feel better when you're not feeling good about yourself.

How you express yourself is a true impression of who you really are and how you actually feel. The first impression is everlasting. If we look back and say we were having a bad day, it truly will not matter. The damage is done. Your energy did the greeting before you did. Your energy says more than words can. Some spoken words are untrue but your energy always tells the true story.

That's why it's important to network with positive

people from whom you can grow and learn. Eliminating negativity will allow your energy to thrive out into the universe, attracting and connecting your heart's desires.

When you start your day on a positive note, your day will end up on a better note. The next time you have the opportunity to greet someone, ask yourself, how are you going to do so? A nod may work better, with a smile.

Hand Shake

Have you wondered about the people who refuse to shake your hand when you extend yours? Would this offend you? Do you understand why? I assume they're afraid of catching germs. Some of them will probably go out and catch a cold the very next day.

I don't care how old you are or how many your handshakes others have turned down, it still makes you wonder if it's really because of you, doesn't it?

This is a normal reaction to rejection. You look within for fault. I would not attend an affair that didn't involve meeting and greeting someone and shaking a hand or two.

Kiss of Death

Personally, I prefer a handshake over a kiss, especially if I don't know whom I'm kissing. Then again, sometimes we must be careful about receiving a kiss from someone we know more so than from someone we don't know at all.

45

Remember, Jesus was set up by a member of his crew. Judas was one of his disciples who betrayed Jesus by using a kiss to identify Him. From the kiss, Jesus went on to be prosecuted, whipped with 40 lashes and crucified.

After He died, Jesus was buried in a garden in a new sepulcher, where no man had been laid to rest before.

He Has Risen

Jesus rose from the dead and now sits on his throne in Heaven. Earth is His foot stool. Holler! I believe this is so. Don't ever think you're not going to make it in this world. We've got more than enough reasons to **keep it moving**. He has risen.

All in the Plan

The world was framed by the word of God. The Word is God and God is the Word. Everything that breathes— every bird in the air, every fish in the sea, vegetation all living creatures exist because God spoke it into existence. From the ground, God made man and from the rib of man, He created woman.

God knew that man needed **hope**, knowing that the road ahead would be long and dreary for some. He knew many would be in it for themselves, **lacking love**, joy, and passion for others—not willing to help or to share.

Instead of lifting others, these people would deceive others because of their own greed. He knew the world would be corrupt before it was corrupted. God knew man was visual and boastful. So he came up with a plan for us.

Why?

For God so loved the world, he wanted to give people something to believe in. He wanted us to have heaven right here on earth. He knew there would be a lack of love, passion, joy and peace. As a result there would be murder, greed, false accusations, darkness and death.

How?

He needed someone **without blemish** or sin born of the flesh who would walk and talk like ordinary men but with powers to perform miracles unknown to man.

Trust in God and not man. Trust in the **power of God** unknown and never seen by man. He would give his Son enough time to perform miracles, be deceived, get crucified, die on the cross and rise from the dead.

God will find a woman **worthy enough** to have his only begotten son.

What?

He gave his **only begotten son** so we may have life and live it more abundantly. God planned for Jesus to walk in the flesh so that He could be seen among the people on Earth. Leaving witnesses to spread the gospel, sharing all of the miracles they witnessed. From what I recall, Jesus raised Lazarus from the dead, gave evil spirits permission to come out of one man into a herd of more than 2,000 pigs. The lame began to walk, the voiceless began to talk and the blind began to see. Jesus fed thousands with five loaves of bread and two fish.

Where?
He started in **the spirit** and ended up in the flesh on earth.

When?
While hanging on the cross, Jesus saw his mother Mary and the disciples standing by her side.

He said, "Dear woman, here is your son." And to his disciples, he said, "Here is your mother."

After knowing all was done, Jesus thirst for water but was given vinegar instead. After receiving the drink, Jesus said, "It is finished." With that, he bowed his head and gave up his spirit.

Can I Get a Witness?
God knew the procedures to prepare us for the Sabbath. No one would be left hanging. There were two other men who were crucified with Jesus. After breaking one of the men's legs and then the other's, when it was Jesus' turn, they noticed he was already dead. So the soldier pierced

Jesus side with a spear, bringing forth a flow of **blood and water**.

> *"The man that saw this was given testimony. He testifies so that you may believe. These things happened so the scripture would be fulfilled. Not one of his bones will be broken and another scripture they would look on the one they have pierced." –* ***John 19:36-37 NIV.***

Warned Not to Tell

Jesus strictly warned them not to tell this story to anyone. He said, "The son of man must suffer many things and be rejected by the elders, chief priests and teachers of the law, and he must be killed and on the third day be raised to life."

> *"He humbled you, causing you to hunger and then feeding you with manna, which neither you nor your fathers had known, to teach you that man does not live on bread alone but on every word that comes from the* ***mouth*** *of the* ***Lord!****" –* ***Deuteronomy 8:3.***

Are You a Nurtured Artist?

You must plan to live. If you're not growing, you're dying! This is only the beginning. If you started this book as a starving artist, I hope you now feel equipped with the power within to start making changes in your life. I truly want to see you succeed and live out the plan that God has for you.

What's your plan? I truly would like to know. Visit me online at Get More in Life Coaching, LLC, www. getmoreinlifecoaching.com. Please send me an email at info@getmoreinlifecoaching.com or leave a comment on any page within my site.

I love helping people use their own natural abilities to craft the lifestyle of their dreams. I hope we stay in touch!

About the Author

Antreina E. Stone is the founder of Get More in Life Coaching, LLC. Author, business coach, life coach, wife, mother, sister, grandmother, godmother and friend, Antreina started her journey as an entrepreneur when she opened Antreina's Earrings in 1989. Since then, she's managed more than 100 jewelry consultants and sold well over 50,000 pairs of earrings, manufactured by hand and still selling today in boutiques and online at www.antreinasearrings.com. Today, Antreina specializes in helping people live to their full potential. Visit our Coaching Programs page to find out how Antreina can help you to craft the lifestyle of your dreams.

"Are You a Starving Artist?" is Antreina's first book. Look for more books by Antreina as well as coaching programs to help you craft the lifestyle of your dreams at www.getmoreinlifecoaching.com.

www.ingramcontent.com/pod-product-compliance
Lightning Source LLC
Chambersburg PA
CBHW031633040426
42452CB00007B/811